Carb Charts

Low Carb Reference

Book 8 in the
Low Carb Reference Series

Lisa Shea

Amazon paperback ISBN: 9798339869603

Kindle ASIN B0064J8XFA

~ v14 ~

All images are photographed by and copyright to

Lisa Shea

Except cover image which was purchased from iStockPhoto

Please visit LowCarb.BellaOnline.com

For more great recipes for healthy eating!

This book has earned the
BellaOnline seal of approval
and is part of the BellaOnline
publishing library.

Contents

Introduction

Low carb dieting is all about watching the carb counts of your food. We count carbs for a simple reason - foods with low carb counts have low sugar. Foods with high carb counts have high sugar. Sure, you *could* eat corn occasionally because it's tasty - but corn is mostly made up of sugar and water. It has few nutrients. If you fill up on corn, you're filling your stomach full of sugar and have little room left for food with nutrients in it. In essence you're causing malnutrition through stomach-jamming.

The point of following a low carb lifestyle is to treasure your stomach space. You only have a limited amount of food that can fit into your stomach every day. You need to choose wisely so the food you put into your mouth is food that is high in nutrients and vitamins while low in sugar. It's a balancing act. Knowing a food's carb count helps you find that balance.

It's important not to obsess over the carb count of an exact portion. Is it 5.2g or 5.5g? In reality, the carb count of *any* food varies in many different ways. Scientists have determined a "general" count for tomatoes, for example. But is it a roma tomato, a plum tomato, a big sandwich tomato, or a cherry tomato? Is it a big roma tomato or a little roma tomato? Is it a roma tomato grown in California, or a roma tomato grown in Louisiana? Was the tomato grown in the cool days of spring or the hot days of summer? All of these differences impact the sugar count of the food. You are *never* going to have exact counts. The idea is to get into a "low range" instead of a "high range".

Be sure to vary your diet. Broccoli is great for you - but eating a diet of 100% broccoli would cause severe malnutrition. Make sure you draw foods from all the different food groups, and explore new types of foods. There's a ten-try rule in taste - while your taste buds might originally reject a new food as being "icky", after a few times of eating it, your taste buds learn to adapt. It's a survival thing. Your taste buds figure that if this is all it's going to get to keep its body fed, it might as well learn to like it.

There are many delicious foods out there that your parents may never have exposed you to. Your childhood may have put your taste buds at a disadvantage. Learn to like a variety of foods, and you can literally go years on a low carb diet without ever eating the same dish twice!

I'll note that carb counts for a given food item should be the same no matter where you look them up. These are scientific values. The carb count for a 12oz apple should be within a certain range, no matter which scientist tests it. There will be a slight variation depending on the specific apple, its ripeness, and so on, but the values should be within a reasonably small range.

This book here is a compilation of known scientific values for a wide variety of items, which I have organized and presented for you. If you have any suggestions about the layout, please let me know! I'm quite open to feedback. Also, let me know what other supplemental information you'd find helpful in this book, beyond the basic foundation information I provide next.

Why Buy This Book

Food carb charts are comprised of scientific facts; this data can be found at the USDA website. This book is meant to supplement that online database. We all end up in locations where we lose web access. This book allows you to maintain access to the important carb information during those times so you can still make healthy choices.

People who say "I can just look up every item on the web with lightning-fast results" must have far better phones and connectivity than I do, especially in some of the restaurants and farmer's markets I visit! I wrote this book as much for my own use as for helping the low carb community. I use this book all the time myself.

Also, unlike an online database which just gives that one item's values, I portioned all of the data out so you can easily compare "apples and oranges" (grin) and make wiser choices. Instead of having to go back and forth between individual item pages through a database-driven system, you can peruse all your options in a given category and know which item will best suit your current dietary needs.

The introductory articles I provide help ground newcomers in the concepts of effective vs total carbs and how a glycemic index works. These are all important foundations for a healthy eater to understand.

Finally, for those who drink alcohol, I put a substantial amount of effort in researching, testing, and updating the drink carb chart values. Many of these data sets involved me personally writing and communicating with the manufacturers of the alcohols involved. So this information is the result of a careful investigation. Now the results are at your fingertips!

Please let me know if there are any additional items you'd like to have carb values for. I am continually working on improving and expanding my information here, so it best helps you live a healthy lifestyle!

Ebook vs Print Book Versions

If you buy the print book version of this, I can send you the matching ebook version. Even if you're a print-book reader, I highly recommend you get that free ebook version.

If you did buy this in ebook format, that's wonderful. Here's why.

Search is Built In
Whatever ebook version you are using, you should have instant access to a 'search' feature. Apparently based on some reviews I've read, some ebook-reading people don't know that they can search an ebook! Searching an ebook is one of the best reasons for HAVING an ebook.

Look at your reader or app you're using if this is an ebook version. I am absolutely sure it has a 'search' button. That's why most ebooks don't bother with an index. Why have an index when the person can instantly search for exactly what they need?

You can Add Notes
Is there a specific type of food that matters to you? With ebooks you can easily add notes and comments to your book. That way you can find those foods easily and remember what your thoughts are on them. Make your own customized comments to help the book become even more useful to you.

You can Always Have It With You
Some people don't realize that they can read Kindle books on their PC and smartphone. That SmashWords books are available in Kindle format. Whatever readers you own, think beyond their physical confines.

Tuck a copy of the book on your phone. Your PC. Other systems. That way the data is available whenever you need it.

If you're having challenges figuring out all the way ebooks can work, feel free to contact me. I'm happy to lend a hand. It'll help you not only with this particular book but with your entire library of reading material.

Why are Carbs Given in Grams?

First, let's start very simple. A gram is a *measure of weight*. You probably get all sorts of things given to you in grams. For example, gold is usually sold by the gram. Beads are often sold by the gram. Most of the world uses grams as their measurement standard; only the US, Liberia, and Burma still use ounces. One gram is only 0.04 ounces, so you can see why grams are so much better for careful measurement! A gram is *far* more precise.

So, in terms of eating healthily, all nutrition labels give their values in grams, and people using countertop food scales set those to measure in grams. That gives you the most detailed weight of the items you are weighing and eating.

Here is a sample nutrition label, for a box of sugar-free candies. What they are saying here is that if you ingest 16 grams of candies, that you will be ingesting 14g of sugar alcohols. Everything is indicated by the gram of weight.

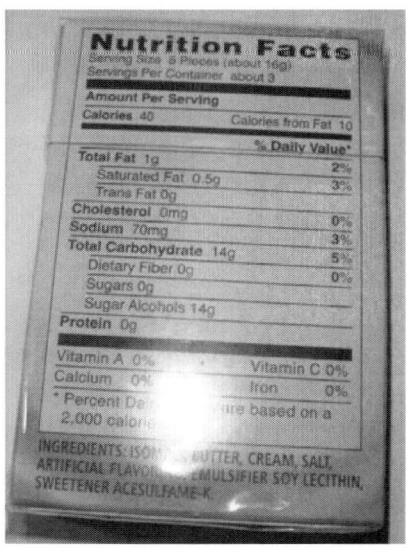

This is exactly how the Low Carb system works. They have you counting the grams of carbs you ingest every day and keeping track of that. So you need to know how many grams of carbs are in each item you eat and add them up as you go.

Why are Carbs Listed by the Gram?
Again, a gram is a small measurement of weight. This is *by far* the easiest way for nutritionists to help you know what you are

ingesting. If they tried to do it "by the ounce" for example it would be a nightmare. Who would be adding up 0.04oz of carbs in their tomato plus 0.001oz of carbs in their celery? Grams are far easier to work with. That is why the entire world - including the US - uses grams for all their nutrition information.

Why Provide Values by Weight and not by Serving?
Nutrition information is provided to help you make healthy choices about the food you are making. There are few healthy diets out there - regardless of their basis - that want you to eat processed food. Processed foods might have easy to read nutrition labels, since they have already determined the recipe for you, added up all the ingredients, and dumped out the results. But the end results are usually full of sodium, preservatives, and other unwanted items. The goal of pretty much every healthy eating system is for you to make fresh food at home, using quality ingredients. It's cheaper too!

So that being said, a nutritionist would have NO idea what specific recipe you are cooking, to be able to say "the amount of zucchini in your final serving is going to be X". Maybe your zucchini recipe today calls for 24g of zucchini plus 24g of tomatoes and is a "veggie medley." Maybe the recipe for tomorrow calls for 42g of zucchini and is a "zucchini with garlic"! Every recipe is going to be different. Every recipe uses different proportions of ingredients. There is no way any nutritionist would know how much zucchini you were using in your serving of food, to be able to say "the total carb grams in your final serving is going to be X." It all depends on how *much* zucchini you are using. That quantity is typically measured by weight.

That is why carb counts provide values based on grams of each ingredient. That way you can calculate exactly what you are ingesting. If you make a mix of 100g tomato, 100g zucchini, 100g onion and sauté it with garlic, you simply plug in the values of the carbs in each amount.

To go along with this concept, it's also important to keep in mind that there is no such thing as a "standard serving" that every single human being eats. If you have a tuna steak with lunch, you might have a 113g steak. If you have a tuna steak with dinner, you might eat a 226g steak. A child might have a "standard serving" of 60g of steak! All of these are the individuals' normal, healthy serving. That is why everything in the nutrition world is done by weight. It lets you know exactly what you are eating, exactly what its nutritional values are, and accurately measure out what you are ingesting.

In the world of low carb, we do not count a mythical "serving size" (which as mentioned does not exist across all ages and genders). You eat slowly, with awareness, until you are full, and then you stop. You do not stuff yourself, but you do not go hungry either. You listen to your body's message. So "serving size" is not a consideration at all. It is about eating healthy food, eating until you are full, and counting the carbs you ingest.

As always, feel free to contact me if you have any questions about these nutrition basics! These basics apply to *all* eating - not just low carb. Understanding grams and what they are about is critical to every person who wants to be able to read a nutritional label and know what it means.

Why Aren't There Lines in the Charts?

I have to admit, this is one of the most bizarre complaints I've gotten about this book. A few readers complained that instead of having grids with lines in my results information, I show the information without lines.

The reason why has to do with ebooks.

Most ebook formats do NOT ALLOW table structures. That's because older versions of readers could not handle tables. Therefore, to make sure this book could be read on all versions of all readers, I had to eliminate tables with lines. I had to show the charts in a simple format without lines.

The few entries you see in these pages that have lines and grids had to be done with graphics. Graphics are the only consistent way to show information like that.

Graphics can't be searched, though. So if I made all the information in graphic format, there'd be no way for people to search for data by item name.

So this is a trade-off we make in our ebook world. We show information in the way it is most accessible to people.

If the lack of lines and squares in my charts upsets you, I apologize profusely. But it's a necessity of layout in order to be able to reach all readers.

Why Isn't It One Giant Alphabetical List?

Some readers would prefer just having one massive long list of everything in alphabetical order.

Here's why I didn't do that.

First, everyone should have access to the ebook version of this book. Either you bought the ebook version directly or, when you bought the paperback version, it gave you free access to the ebook version as a bonus. Either way, you can now easily search for any word you want and jump immediately to that word. It is instantaneous and easy. Indexing every single food item in the list would add enormous amounts of pages to the back of this book and the process would be slow and tedious to use it.

Second, a key feature of this book is that you can easily compare "like items". If you are looking at having a meat protein in your meal, you can easily look at that one area and see how the options compare. If you're looking to have a veggie side dish, you can see all the veggies at a glance and decide which is best suited for you.

With a giant alphabetical list, you have the exact same problem you have if you do one-item searches in a USDA database. You get the information in isolation. You learn the details of that one particular thing, but it doesn't give you a more holistic idea of how that item fits into the world of options.

Why Doesn't It Show Fiber / Sugar Alcohol / Etc. Values?

When we discuss the content which is actually in a food item, there is FAR more than just that one net carb value for a food item. For example, here's details for a cup of canned corn.

Nutrition Facts		
Serving Size 1 cup (256 g)		
Amount Per Serving		
Calories 164		Calories from Fat 0
		% Daily Value*
Total Fat 0 g		0%
Saturated Fat 0 g		0%
Trans Fat g		
Cholesterol 0 mg		0%
Sodium 545 mg		23%
Total Carbohydrate 38 g		13%
Dietary Fiber 3 g		12%
Sugars 5 g		
Protein 3 g		
Vitamin A	7%	. Calcium 1%
Vitamin C	17%	. Iron 0%
		. Potassium 12%

*Percent Daily Values are based on a 2,000 calorie diet. Your daily values may be higher or lower depending on your calorie needs:

	Calories	2,000	2,500
Total Fat	Less than	65g	80g
Sat Fat	Less than	20g	25g
Cholesterol	Less than	300mg	300mg
Sodium	Less than	2,400mg	2,400mg
Total Carbohydrate		300g	375g
Dietary Fiber		25g	30g

Calories per gram:
Fat 9 . Carbohydrate 4 . Protein 4

Lots of that is important in a holistic sense. It's good to know the calorie count. It's good to know how much fiber is in there. It's helpful to know the specific sugar count. Sometimes foods have sugar alcohols – that's also useful to know. And the protein value is important for many people. As is the amount of trans fats.

Then how about sodium? Sodium is critical to watch.

But you can see what is happening here.

As you add each data point in, the page becomes far harder to scan and get information from. Now you're not glancing down a chart and figuring out which vegetable is best while you stand in a supermarket aisle. Now you're digging through lots of data which takes time to decipher.

There are plenty of books out there that provide that level of complicated detail. There's no need to re-invent the wheel.

This book here has a specific focus. It looks at the net carbs each item has, in a way that you can easily compare that food item with its similar neighbors.

If you really need to know the fiber values of foods for medical reasons, or the salt levels, then I apologize. This book probably won't be a good match for you. But in terms of quickly and easily knowing which items fall within your net carb ranges, this book should do the trick!

Food Carb Charts

Carb charts are by their nature generic. They aim to scientifically determine a mid-range number which can apply to all items within a given food category, like "apple" or "carrot," regardless of where it was grown or what particular type it is.

A carb chart value is not exact number down to the hundredths of a point. These numbers should be taken as a guideline, to help you choose the healthier foods rather than the sugar-rich foods.

Beans

Beans are a staple of many diets in regions where animal protein (chicken, beef, etc.) is hard to come by. They are great for hard working farmers, because they pack a lot of calories in a small package. While this is ideal for people slaving in the fields ten hours a day, it's less healthy for people sitting in an office chair.

The carbs listed are the effective carbs - the fiber counts have already been removed. Servings are 1/2 cup.

Please note this serving is a half cup of *cooked* beans. Beans swell up when they cook.

Adzuki beans – 19.5g
Baked beans - 18g
Black beans – 13g
Chickpeas / garbanzo beans - 21.5g
Fava beans - 21g
Green beans - 2.9g
Hyacinth beans - 19.5g
Kidney beans - 28g
Lentil beans - 22g
Lima beans - 12g
Mung beans - 7g
Navy beans - 24g
Pink beans – 19g
Pinto beans - 14.5g
Refried beans - 12g
Snap beans - 2g
Soy beans - 8.5g
Split peas - 20.5g
White beans - 23g
Winged beans - 12g

If you have any type of bean not on this list that you'd like to know about, please let me know! I am happy to research and update this listing. That is true for all charts in this book.

Berry

Berries are one of *the* most important things you can eat on any diet - whether you're choosing to eat low carb, low glycemic index, or any other style of menu. Berries are full of antioxidants and nutrients.

Try to get berries into your weekly meal plan!

All berry counts given here are for 1/4 cup, except where noted. They are effective carb counts, with the fiber already removed.

acai berry (1oz) - 5g
blackberries - 2.7g
blueberries - 4.1g
boysenberries – 2.5g
cloudberries (100g) – 8g
cranberries - 2.0g
currant - 4g
elderberries - 4g
goji berry (5 Tbsp) - 21g
gooseberries - 9g
huckleberries (100g) - 8g
loganberry (100g) – 8g
mulberries – 3g
pokeberry shoots - 1g
raspberries - 1.5g
salmonberry (100g) – 8g
strawberries - 1.8g

Bread

Bread is a great source of fiber if you eat healthy bread. However, it can be a source of empty carbs / calories with little nutrition if you buy over-processed white bread. Choose wisely!

Remember, low carb isn't about "avoid all carbs!" It is about eating healthy carbs and avoiding junk food that gives lots of carbs with no nutrition. White bread definitely falls into the junk food category.

Carb values are shown for 1 slice of bread, except where noted. All carbs shown are effective carbs. The fiber has already been subtracted.

bagel, plain (4" diameter) – 54g
banana bread – 31g
challah – 11g
cornbread – 28g
focaccia – 27g
Irish soda bread (100g) – 54g
Italian bread – 38g
muffin, plain (3.5oz) – 48g
oatmeal bread – 12g
potato bread – 17g
pumpernickel bread - 12g
rye bread - 13.7g
seven grain bread (Pepperidge Farm) - 5g
sourdough bread - 14g
wheat bread (Wonder bread) - 8g
white bread - 12.2g

Cheese

Cheese is a delicious, nutritious food. It is in essence milk from a cow (or sheep, goat, etc.) that has been processed and solidified. Therefore, cheese is full of calcium and protein. It's naturally filling.

Cheese can make just about any meal very tasty. It's a perfect snack, too! Just don't put it on bland bread. Try it on a slice of cucumber or on a pepperoni ring!

Here are carb charts for various types of cheese. Unless otherwise noted, all amounts are for 2 Tbsp. That's about three slices of the type that goes onto crackers (small squares).

All values are net carbs. There's no fiber in cheese ;).

American (one burger slice) - 0.3g
Asiago - 0.4g
Blue - 0.4g
Brick (1oz) – 1g
Brie (1 sq. inch) – 0.1g
Camembert (1 sq. inch) – 0.1g
Cheddar - 0.2g
Cheshire (1oz) – 1g
Colby (1oz) - 0.7g
Colby Jack (1oz) - 0.5g
Cream - 0.8g
Feta - 0.8g
Fontina - 0.2g
Goat - 0.3g
Gruyere - 0.1g
Limburger – 0.1g
Mascarpone (1oz) – 1.0g
Monterey Jack - 0.1g

Mozzarella - .3g
Muenster - .2g
Parmesan - .3g
Ricotta (1 oz) – 1.5g
Swiss - .5g

Note: While cheese has low carbs, it's also important to eat it in moderation. Eating giant blocks of cheese will cause a variety of issues for your body. Like constipation …

Cheese - Cottage

I adore cottage cheese. I'm keeping this separate from the main
cheese category because in modern times cottage cheese comes in
a wildly varying group of styles. It is one of the few cheeses that
comes in different levels specifically aimed at dieters.

Most cheese comes as a unit. It can be a hard clock, like most
cheddars, or it can be a soft style, like brie. But either way the
cheese is consistent.

Cottage cheese is different. The cheese isn't "pressed together"
with cottage cheese – the natural curds are allowed to stay
separate. So it's more like bunches of globules than one solid
pudding-like consistency.

When you buy cottage cheese in a store you can get a wide variety
of styles. Large curd. Small curd. No sugar added. Low fat. So
there isn't just one standard cottage cheese set of nutrition. It really
is brand by brand.

Here's just a few of the options, so you can see the ranges.

Brand	Style	Serving	Net Carbs
Hood	Country style	½ cup	5g
Hood	Low fat w/peaches	½ cup	17g
Breakstone	Small curd 2%	½ cup	5g
Breakstone	Large curd 4%	½ cup	6g
Daisy	Regular 4%	½ cup	4g
Daisy	Low fat 2%	½ cup	4g

As you can see, once you start adding in items the values can change dramatically. So if you're going for cottage cheese it's a good idea to stay with the basics and then only add in items you really want to have in there.

Condiments

Whether it's garlic, pickles, ketchup or other "things" you add to your meals, condiments often come with a carb and calorie cost. It's important that these values are added into your daily intake and accounted for. Here are the carb counts for many of your favorite condiments.

Most values here are for 1 tablespoon unless otherwise indicated. The carbs stated are effective carbs.

Capers: 0.1g
Chili sauce: 5g
Chutney: 5.9g
Garlic (1): 0.9g
Ginger slide: 0.8g
Honey (1 tsp): 5.8g
Ketchup: 4.0g
Maple syrup: 13.4g
Mayonnaise: 3.5g
Mustard, Dijon: 0.5g
Mustard, yellow: 0.6g
Olives, black: 0.7g
Olives, green: 2.5g
Olive oil: 0g
Pepper (1 tsp): 0.3g
Pickle (1): 1.9g
Relish: 6g
Salt: 0g
Soy sauce: 0.9g
Special Sauce (McDonald's Big Mac): 3g
Steak Sauce (A-1): 3g
Worcestershire sauce (1 tsp): 0.9g

Vinegar is listed separately, on a page of its own, because there are a variety of options with it.

Cream

Are you confused about heavy cream, whipping cream, half and half, clotted cream and other types found in recipes? This easy to use chart explains them all, along with their carb values.

Cream is a key component of many low carb recipes because the fat in cream gives foods a delicious flavor and texture. This chart shows the percentage fat, so if for example you have Double Cream and need Heavy Cream, you know how much to dilute it.

Note that all of these values are averages. Check your particular brand of cream to find out the carbs per serving on it. Cream is in essence a component of cow milk (and milk from other animals). When a farmer milks a cow, they let the liquid sit. The cream "rises to the top" as the cliché says and is skimmed off. Depending on the fat content of that cream, it is given different names.

Higher fat creams tend to taste better, have a richer texture, and don't curdle as easily when used in cooking.

Cream	US Fat	England Fat	Carbs / cup
Clotted cream		55%	
Double cream		48%	
Heavy cream	36%		6g
Whipping cream	30%	35%	7g
Whipped cream		35%	7g
Single cream / Light cream	18%	18%	8g
Half cream / Half and Half	12%	12%	8g

Sour cream occurs when regular cream is fermented. A cup of sour cream has 7g of carbs.

Fruit

While fruits can be a special, sweet treat, you should be cautious about gorging on fruits while on a low carb diet. Those apple and orange treats are full of sugar! Others, like watermelon, are perfect.

Portions are 1/4 cup unless otherwise indicated. Carbs shown are effective / net carbs; the fiber was already removed.

Note that fruit juices are usually chock full of sugars. Read the labels carefully, because it's usually much better to drink water than to drink any fruit juices. Berries were listed earlier in this book.

apple (1) - 17.3g
applesauce - 6.2g
apricot (1) - 3.1g
avocado (1) – 5.0g
banana (1) - 21.2g
cantaloupe - 3.0g
carambola / starfruit (1) - 3g
chayote (1) – 6g
cherries - 4.2g
coconut - 1.3g
grapes - 6.7g
grapefruit (1) – 9g
honeydew – 3.6g
kiwi (1) – 6.5g
lemon (1) - 3.8g
mango - 6.3g
orange (1) - 12.9g
papaya (1 small) – 14g
passion fruit (1) - 2g
peach (1) - 8.9g
pear (1) - 21.1g

pineapple - 4.3g
plantain - 12g
plum (1) - 7.6g
pomegranate (1) - 40g
raisins - 31.0g
watermelon - 2.6g

Fruit Juice

Fruit juices are in general a sugar-rich product. The manufacturers take the fiber rich fruit, leave behind all the fiber, and all you get are the fruit sugars and colors.

Sad to say, the carb counts on many fruit juices are similar to that of regular Coke, which has 30g carbs per 8oz glass! In addition, the acids are known to eat away at your teeth, causing them to decay more quickly. All in all, it's far better to eat the raw fruit, to get its full fiber and nutrition.

I include some vegetable juices in this listing to help provide a comparison.

These counts are all net carbs. All are 8oz servings.

acerola juice – 8g
apple juice, unsweetened - 29g
carrot juice - 24g
cranberry juice - 36g
grape juice - 19g
grapefruit juice - 11g
lemon juice - 20g
lime juice - 23.5g
orange juice - 26g
passion fruit juice - 32g
pineapple juice - 34g
pomegranate juice - 32g
prune juice - 40g
tangerine juice - 24g
tomato juice - 5g
V-8 juice - 10g
watermelon juice – 16g

Lettuce

Lettuce is the core of most salads. It is fresh, nutritious, filling, full of water, and helps hold together your other salad items. Try to have two salads a day!

Butterhead Lettuce
Butterhead lettuce is a group that includes Boston and Bibb styles of lettuce. It has loose leaves. A cup has 1g of carbs. You get 78% of your vitamin A.

Iceberg Lettuce
Iceberg lettuce is the first type of lettuce that most people encounter. It is the round ball shaped lettuce that is very crisp and crunchy, and used frequently in salads and on burgers. It's generally pretty cheap. It's only 0.4g of carbs for an entire cup of lettuce, as in not even 1g. Many salads are a serving of iceberg lettuce plus a few tomatoes and cukes, then salad dressing. On the downside, iceberg lettuce has little flavor and not much nutrition. So this is a good way to get you started on salads, if you're not used to them, but try to "move up" from iceberg when you can.

Radicchio Lettuce
This lettuce isn't actually a lettuce, it's a chicory leaf. It's shaped in a ball like an iceberg, but is a reddish-purple color rather than green. It's got a strong bitter-spicy flavor to it and is usually served with fruit salads rather than as a standalone veggie salad. You don't get a lot of nutrition here - for the 2g of carbs per cup, you only get 5% Vitamin C, 1% iron, and not much else.

Red Leaf Lettuce
As you might imagine, this lettuce type has a slightly red tint to its leaves. It's only 1g of carbs per cup and you get 42% of your vitamin A, as well as 2% vitamin C, 2% iron, and 1% calcium.

Romaine Lettuce

Romaine is the dark, "fluffy" lettuce type - less crisp than iceberg, but containing *far* more nutrition. You get 75% your daily serving of Vitamin K with a single cup, along with 30% of your Vitamin A, 22% Vitamin C and much more. It's very good for you. It's only 0.9g of carbs per serving. So a tiny bit more carbs than iceberg - but far better for you health wise. I highly recommend getting a daily romaine salad into your normal eating habits. Romaine is also known as "Cos" lettuce.

Spinach

OK Spinach is different than lettuce, but you can just as easily make a spinach salad and it is *full* of nutrients. It's slightly more carby - about 1.2g per cup. There's a reason that Popeye ate this for super strength. You get 140% of your Vitamin A, 50% of your Vitamin C, 40% of your iron, 12% of your calcium, and much, much more. I would have a regular salad and then a main course of spinach in some form. This stuff is perfect for you.

Swiss Chard

Related to the beet, the Swiss chard leaves are nicely nutritious. You get 1g of carbs, 44% of your vitamin A, 18% of your vitamin C, plus 4% iron and 2% calcium. The flavor is similar to spinach.

Kale

Related to cabbage, Kale has been adored since the Middle Ages for its powerhouse of strength. A cup of kale provides 5.4g of carbs with 1.3g of fiber. It has a half-gram of fat, 2.2g of protein, and a whopping 684% of your Vitamin K. Add that in with 206% of your Vitamin A and 134% of your Vitamin C, and you can see why the carbs are worth it.

Meat and Poultry

Meat consumption has always been important for women, to keep their iron levels up. The Atkins diet is perfect for meat lovers, since most meat is zero carb! Servings are 6oz.

Keep in mind that "meat products" often have sugars added into them to sweeten the taste, and that adds in carbs. That would include hot dogs and kielbasa.

Bacon - .1g
Bison - 0g
Calf Liver - 10.4g
Caribou - 0g
Chicken - 0g
Cornish Game Hen - 0g
Deer / venison - 0g
Duck - 0g
Frankfurter / hot dog (1) - 2g
Goose - 0g
Ground beef - 0g
Hamburger – 0g
Guinea hen - 0g
Kielbasa - .8g
Lamb – 0g
Moose – 0g
Pheasant - 0g
Pork - 0g
Quail - 0g
Sausage - 2g
Spam (2oz) - 2g
Steak - 0g
Turkey - 0g
Veal Steak - 0g

Deli Slices
Bologna - .7g
Ham - 1.5g
Pastrami - 2.6g
Roast Beef - 2.3g
Salami - 2.4g

Being on an Atkins or low carb diet is not a license to eat bacon every day and hotdogs every night. You still need to eat healthily!

Most low carb diets recommend only one serving of bacon a week, for salt and other reasons.

Most healthy diets of all styles recommend avoiding hotdogs because of the nitrate level in them. Excessive nitrates are linked to diabetes and other serious diseases.

Stores do now offer hot dots and sandwich meats in a nitrate free variety. I highly recommend you seek them out and use them if you want to keep eating these types of meats. It will be good for your health.

Seafood and fish is separate on its own page.

Milk and Dairy

Many adults develop lactose intolerance; your body naturally loses its ability to process milk as it ages. Many diets cut down your milk intake at the start to test for this.

Even if you've done a milk allergy test before, it might be good to try it again. Bodies change over time! Cut out dairy products for two weeks straight. See how you feel. You might notice a drop in bloating and other allergic reactions which you had not realized were related to milk.

All carb counts are given for effective carbs. Fiber has already been removed.

Milk Products
all milk values are given in 1 cup servings.

Whole milk - 11.4g
2% fat milk - 11.7g
1% fat milk - 11.7g
fat free milk - 11.9g
Kefir (fermented milk) – 9g
Milk is a natural substance. You should always check the label of the milk you are buying, to see what the carb count in your milk is. There are variations from brand to brand.

Dairy Products
butter - 0g
egg (1) - 0.6g
half and half (2 Tbsp) - 1.0g
heavy cream (2 Tbsp) - 0.8g
mayonnaise (1 tsp) - 0.1g
sour cream (2 Tbsp) - 1.2g

In general, the heavier the cream or milk, the better (lower) the carb count.

A note about lactose intolerance and milk allergies. They are two separate things. For people who are lactose intolerant, their bodies cannot process the lactose (natural milk sugars) found in milk. However, for people who are allergic to milk, they are having a histamine reaction to the proteins in the milk. In either situation, of course, it's a wise idea to avoid drinking milk.
While cheese is a dairy product, because there are so many types of cheese they are kept on a separate list. Cream is also listed separately.

Milk - Yogurt

Yogurt is what results when you take milk and add in bacteria to ferment it. Traditional cow-milk yogurt ends up with a tart flavor as a result.

You can also get "Greek Yogurt" which is a strained version. This removes the whey and lactose, resulting in a mix which is less tart, less carby, has less sodium, and more protein.

The carb counts of yogurt therefore varies wildly depending on what style you have an how it's been made. Here are just a few options in the yogurt world. It pays to look at the container of what you're about to buy.

Brand	Style	Serving	Net Carbs
Oikos Triple-Zero	Mixed berry	150g	8g
Yoplait Original	Strawberry	Container	25g
Yoplait thick/creamy	Peaches & cream	Container	31g
Chiobani fruit-bottom	Banana	150g	14g
Chiobani plain	Non-fat	150g	6g

Nuts and Seeds

Nuts and Seeds are both good and bad for dieters. They are intense little packets of protein, but some are quite rich in carbs as well. Choose wisely!

All counts are given for 2 Tbsp of nuts, unless noted. The values shown are effective carb counts. The fiber values have been removed already.

The best way to eat nuts is to pour out the portion into a serving dish and put the rest away. That way you feel full with what you have, without being lured by the rest of the container.

Acorns (100g) - 40g
Almonds - 1.4g
Beech nuts (1oz) - 9g
Butternuts (100g) – 8g
Brazil nuts (1oz) - 1g
Cashews - 5g
Chestnuts - 24.2g
Coconut - 0.7g
Hazelnuts - 1.2g
Macadamia Nuts - 0.9g
Peanut Butter - 4.3g
Peanuts - 1.8g
Pecans - 0.6g
Pine Nuts - 1.7g
Pistachio Nuts - 3.1g
Pumpkin Seeds - 2.4g
Sunflower Seeds - 1.5g
Walnuts - 1.1g

Onions

Do you love onions? They add amazing flavor to a variety of dishes. Here are carb counts for different types of onion and suggestions for uses of each one.

Onions are actually types of lilies and have been used in cooking for at least 7,000 years. They are one of our oldest food sources. Many societies felt onions brought strength and courage, and they were a favorite food of armies.

Onions add a great flavor to recipes and are also antioxidants. Onions have potassium and vitamin C in them. Some studies even show that eating half an onion each day can raise your HDL levels by 30%.

Onions are *very* healthy for you. It's worth it to incorporate them into your diet plans. Toss them on burgers, add them to your salads, and look for recipes that feature onions as a main component.

The one onion type to be cautious with is shallots. These sweet onions can be fairly high in carbs.

All values shown are for a half cup.

Green Onions / Scallions
It is the green "leaves" of this onion that are eaten. The bright green tops are used as decoration in soups, salads and vegetable dishes.
Total Carbs - 4g
Fiber - 1g
Net Carbs - 3g

Italian Red Onion

These colorful onions are often used in salads to add a lively color to them - either a ring or two laid on top, or diced red cubes are tossed over the top of the salad. Italian Reds can be sweet like a Vidalia or more mild. These are usually served raw in salads.
Total Carbs - 5g
Fiber - 1g
Net Carbs - 4g

Pearl Onion

Pearl onions are small, white onions that are often used in beef stews and other meat dishes. They have a mild flavor and are usually served whole, cooked in the sauce or juice of a dish.
Total Carbs - 5g
Fiber - 1g
Net Carbs - 4g

Shallots

Shallots are a sweeter style of onion. They provide a more delicate flavor.
Total Carbs - 16.8g
Fiber - 0g
Net Carbs - 16.8g

Vidalia Onion

One of the most popular onions is a sweet variety first grown in Georgia. It was named after a city there that hosted a large Farmer's Market. Vidalias are the style used in "blooming onions" and are usually used in this manner or in onion rings. A whole Vidalia is usually around 1 cup.
Total Carbs - 5g
Fiber - 1g
Net Carbs - 4g

Yellow Onion
The staple in many traditional recipes, yellow onions are cut into cubes and plunked along with meat dishes. They're used in soups and casseroles. They are usually not very flavorful but are quite inexpensive.
Total Carbs - 5g
Fiber - 1g
Net Carbs - 4g

Pasta Grains Rice

On a low carb diet pasta, grains, and rice are carbs to indulge in only occasionally. They give little nutrition and a ton of 'easy energy' to your body. While this is great for a farmer who works hard in a field, it's less helpful for the average office worker

Most values are given for 1/2 cup of the food, unless noted. All carbs shown are effective carbs.

Buckwheat – 14g
Bulgur Wheat - 12.8g
Corn chips (100g serving) - 58g
Cornmeal (1 Tbsp) - 10.6g
Couscous - 17.1g
Cream of Wheat - 14.3g
Flour (1 Tbsp) - 11.5g
Gnocchi – 15.1g
Millet - 26.8g
Oatmeal - 10.6g
Pasta, egg noodles - 19g
Pasta, shells - 20g
Pasta, spinach - 15.9g
Pasta, whole wheat - 16.6g
Pasta, regular - 18.6g
Potato chips (100g serving) - 49g
Quinoa - 17g
Rice, basmati - 22.5g
Rice, brown - 20.6g
Rice, fried - 28g
Rice, white - 21.9g
Rice, wild - 16g
Tortilla chips (100g serving) - 63g

If you find yourself hit with a strong pasta craving, try going for a pasta soup instead, mixed with veggies or meats. That way the soup fills you up, you get a few pasta items in it, and that will soothe the craving.

About Pasta Servings

Every nutrition label you read (at least in the United States) is *always* shown in serving sizes, in what you are ingesting. So if your pasta box says that a given serving is 20g of carbs, and that a serving size is 1/2 cup, then that is a half cup of *edible* pasta. They are telling you how much you should eat for a serving, and the effect that food will have on your body.

Sometimes they will tell you *in addition* how much dry pasta you need to start with in order to create that edible portion. But that is always secondary information. The nutrition information is for what you will ingest; what is sitting on your plate ready to put into your mouth.

So all of these values are the same thing. They are the amount you are about to eat, in a ready to-eat pile on your plate.

Seafood

If you're into seafood, here's a carb chart to help you determine what seafood items will work well on your low carb or Atkins diet. Seafood can be full of omega-3 oils which are important for healthy brain functioning.

In general, seafood is completely carb free! Just remember to order or prepare the fish grilled or steamed, and not breaded. All servings are 6oz in size.

Fish
Anchovies in Oil - 0g
Bass - 0g
Bluefish - 0g
Carp - 0g
Catfish - 0g
Cod - 0g
Flounder - 0g
Halibut - 0g
Herring - 0g
Mackerel - 0g
Mahi mahi - 0g
Monkfish - 0g
Pollock – 0g
Roughy - 0g
Salmon - 0g
Scrod - 0g
Shad - 0g
Snapper - 0g
Sturgeon - 0g
Swai – 0g
Swordfish - 0g
Tilapia – 0g
Trout - 0g

Tuna - 0g
Whitefish - 0g

Shellfish
Clams - 8.7g
Crab - 0g
Crawfish - 0g
Lobster - 2.2g
Mussels – 6g
Oysters - 12.5g
Scallops - 3.9g
Shrimp - 0g
Squid – 14g

Fish and Mercury

While it's absolutely critical for you to get those omega-3 oils into your body on a regular basis, it's also important to do this in moderation. Many fish do have small amounts of mercury in them.

Your body can naturally process that mercury when taken in small doses. However, if you were to embark on a diet of all tuna fish, all the time, your body would be less happy with you.

Most doctors recommend eating one to two servings a fish a week - but not twenty servings of fish.

Spice / Herb

Herbs and spices are merely ground up bits of plant or bark. How many carbs could you possibly get from a 1/4 tsp of dried up leaves?

Portions are 1 tsp. Carbs shown are effective carbs, the fiber was already removed.

Anise – 0.6g
Allspice – 1.4g
Basil - 0.3g
Cardamom – 0.6g
Chives – 0g
Cilantro / coriander / Chinese parsley – 0g
Cinnamon - 0.6g
Cloves – 0.6g
Cumin – 0.6g
Curry powder – 1.2g
Dill - 0.4g
Garlic Powder - 1.0g
Nutmeg - 0.6g
Oregano - 0.1g
Paprika - 0.4g
Parsley – 0.1g
Pepper - 0.3g
Rosemary - 0.2g
Sage – 0.4g
Salt - 0.0g
Thyme - 0.3g

I realize this may sound a bit like blasphemy, but I would recommend that you not bother to count in herbs and spices unless you really are pouring them in to your dish. The tiny values will easy fall into your "rounding errors".

Any count you use for any food item is an approximation. That apple might be 22g or it might be 18g depending on how big or small it is, how sugary that variety is, etc. Every food is an approximation. If you start worrying about the 0.1g added by oregano, you are focusing on the tiny details and not the big picture.

I'll also note that while it might seem tempting to eat a ton of salt because it has zero carbs in it, salt is dangerous for your body for other reasons. Go easy on the salt.

Vegetables

Vegetables are one of the most important things to eat in any low carb diet - be it Atkins, South Beach, the Zone, or other variations. Eat those vegetables! The key is to choose vegetables that are not high in natural sugar and starch.

The carbs listed are the effective carbs - the fiber counts have already been removed. When not marked, the servings are 1/2 cup.

Artichoke - 6.9g
Asparagus (6) - 2.4g
Beans, green - 2.9g
Beets – 6.5g
Bok Choy - 0.7g
Broccoli - 1.7g
Brussels Sprouts - 7.6g
Cabbage - 1.1g
Carrot - 5.1g
Cauliflower - 1.5g
Celery - 0.8g
Collard Greens – 3.0g
Corn - 14.1g
Cucumber - 1.8g
Eggplant - 2.0g
Garlic – 1.0g
Jicama – 5g
Lettuce - 0.5g
Mushroom - 1.0g
Onion - 4g
Parsnip - 9g
Peas - 6.5g
Peppers, Green - 3.4g
Peppers, Red - 3.3g
Pickle (1 medium) - 2g

Potato - 14g
Potato, Sweet (1) - 28g
Pumpkin - 6.3g
Radish - 0.5g
Rutabaga - 4.0g
Spinach - 0.2g
Squash, green – 3.3g
Squash, yellow - 1.4g
Tomato - 3.2g
Turnips - 2.3g
Yams - 20g
Zucchini - 3.3g

Types of lettuce and onions are on their own pages.

Vinegar

Vinegar is simply a mix of acid and water. Vinegar is often used in cooking to add a tart, acidic flavor to salads and other foods. Here are the carb values for a variety of types of vinegars.

All values here are for 1 tablespoon. The carbs stated are effective carbs.

Apple cider vinegar / ACV: 0.9g
Balsamic vinegar: 2.3g
Cane vinegar: 0g
Coconut vinegar: 1g
Malt vinegar: 0g
Red wine vinegar: 0g
Rice vinegar: 3.0g
Sherry vinegar: 0.9g
White wine vinegar: 1.5g

Be cautious about using fruit flavored vinegars. Often these have sweet fruit juices added into them for flavor. Be sure to look at the container to determine their full carb count.

Studies indicate that eating vinegar helps you feel full more quickly. It's a good idea to choose a menu which incorporates vinegar into it. It will help you fill up more quickly and feel satisfied for longer.

For example, having oil and vinegar for salad dressing is a perfect way to incorporate vinegar into a daily menu.

There are a wide variety of vinegar options on the market, so experiment with different ones. You might find that different vinegars work with different meal plans, and that your current dishes take on new life when an interesting vinegar is incorporated into them.

Drink Carb Charts

Drinking water is always the most healthy thing you can do, and you should aim for eight glasses a day. Remaining properly hydrated is a critical part of maintaining your body's metabolism.

Still, many people like enjoying an alcoholic beverage with their dinner. The following pages contain guidelines for drinks that won't break your diet!

Alcohol - Summary

If you enjoy a cocktail before dinner, or a glass of wine with your steak, you'll be happy to know that most alcohols are zero carb! This list is for straight alcohols, like beer, wine, gin, and so on.

The carb counts given here are effective carb counts, with the fiber removed. All amounts here are for a 1oz shot, except as indicated.

Absinthe – 0g
Armagnac - 0g
Beer (12 oz) - 12.5g
Bourbon - 0g
Brandy - 0g
Cachaça – 0g
Cognac - 0g
Gin - 0g
Mezcal – 0g
Rum - 0g
Scotch - 0g
Tequila - 0g
Vermouth, Dry - 1.4g
Vermouth, Sweet - 4.5g
Vodka - 0g
Whiskey - 0g
Wine, Red (5 oz) – 3.5g
Wine, White (5 oz) - 0.9g

Note that there are of course mixed drinks that involve fruit juices, sugars, and other sweet concoctions. If you start mixing in sodas or juices for a cocktail, you're racking up the carbs very quickly. Use a diet soda whenever possible!

If you're looking for blends like Kahlua, Bailey's, or other concoctions, check out the Cocktail Liqueur Carb Chart.

Remember that alcohol is still a fuel. Alcohol provides calories to your body and is one of the four types of substances that your body can metabolize into fat, along with carbohydrates, proteins, and fats.

So alcohol is *not* a magical "no weight gain" drink. If you drink more than 1-2 drinks a day, it will have a serious impact on your health and your ability to lose weight. In essence your body will burn up the alcohol first for its energy needs, and then if you have other food digesting in your system as well, that other food is now "left over energy" and will get stored as fat. So the alcohol impedes your body's normal energy burning system.

Beer

Are you a fan of beer? Working on a low carb lifestyle? Here's a comparison chart of the various low carb beers and malt beverages on the market, to help you find one you enjoy!

It's important to note that beer makers are constantly fine tuning their formulas and tweaking the nutritional values in them. Beer values can even vary from location to location. Many low carb beers now list their nutritional information on the label, so always go with what the label says for the final word.

Low carb beers are lighter in flavor. You should do *everything* you can to bring out as much of the beer's flavor as you can. Store the cans/bottles away from sunlight so they do not get skunked. Did you know light can skunk a beer in *Under a Minute*?

For the best flavor, do not drink the beer out of the bottle or can. Pour it into a glass and let the foam settle. It should be served right from the fridge. If you can, store a few beer glasses in the freezer so you can serve your beer in the frosted glass.

Beer	Carb	Cal	% Alc	Oz/ Svg	Notes
Accel	2.4g	89	4%	12oz	fresh
Amstel Light	5g	95	3.5%	12oz	flavorful
Aspen Edge	2.6g	94	4.13	12oz	smooth
Bud Light	6.6g	110	4.2%	12oz	OK
Bud Select	3.1g	99	4.3%	12oz	Impressive!
Bud Select 55	1.9g	55	2.4%	12oz	-
Busch Light	6.7g	110	4.2%	12oz	OK
Coastal Light	3.9g	95	3.6%	12oz	-
Coors Light	5g	102	4.2%	12oz	crisp
Corona Light	5g	105	4.5%	12oz	nice flavor
Edison Light	6.5g	109	4%	12oz	-
Guinness	17.6g	194	6%	12oz	high carb
Heineken Light	6.8g	99	-	12oz	high carb
I.C. Light	2.9g	96	4.2%	12oz	-
Keystone Light	5g	104	4.2%	12oz	smooth
Labatt Blue Light	8g	111	4%	12oz	high carb
Labatt Sterling	2.5g			12oz	

Michelob Light	11.7g	134	4.3%	12oz	high carb
Michelob Ultra	2.6g	95	4.2%	12oz	watery
Michelob Ultra Amber	3.7g	114	5%	12oz	nice flavor
MGD Light	2.4g	64	2.8%	12oz	mild light
Mike's Light Lemonade	6g	84	4%	11.2oz	yummy!
Miller Lite	3.2g	96	4.5%	12oz	watery
Milwaukee's Best Light	3.5g	98	4.5%	12oz	bit bitter
Natural Light	3.2g	95	4.2%	12oz	smooth
Rhinebecker Extra	2.5g	106	5%	11.2oz	metallic
Rock Green Light	2.6g	92	-	12oz	fresh
Sam Adams Light	9.7g	124	-	12oz	high carb
San Mig	3.2g	107	5%	12oz	-
Sapporo Light	8.5g	119	4%	12oz	
Sleeman Clear	2.5g				
Thin Ice	1g	90	4.2%	12oz	Ginger Aley

Cocktail Liqueurs

Looking to make cocktails with triple sec, Bailey's, Grand
Marnier, or other non-straight-alcohol substances? Here are the
carb counts for your ingredients. Each count is for 1oz of the drink.
All carb counts given are effective carbs.

Amaretto – 17g - Italian made from apricot pits, tastes like
almonds
Anisette – 11g - Italian from anise seed, licorice flavored
Baileys – 5.5g - Irish blend of cream and whiskey
Carolan's – 6.5g - Irish blend of cream and whiskey
Chambord – 11g - French berry, tastes like raspberries
Chartreuse – 11g - French herbal bend of 130 plants
Cointreau – 10g - style of curacao, orange flavored alcohol
Curacao – 9.6g - orange flavored alcohol from Caribbean
Drambuie – 9g - Scotch whiskey with honey
Frangelico – 11g - Italian liqueur made from hazelnuts
Galliano – 8g – Italian sweet herbal liqueur
Grand Marnier – 11g - French brandy-based orange-flavored
liqueur
Kahlua – 17g - Mexican with coffee flavor
Midori – 11g - Mexican with honeydew melon flavor
Schnapps, Peach – 12g - alcohol distilled from fruit
Southern Comfort – 3g - peach flavored neutral grain alcohol
Triple Sec – 12.5g - style of curacao, orange flavored alcohol

Note I get email from people saying Midori is Japanese, and I used
to think that as well, but the bottles I see clearly say it's made in
Mexico :). So maybe they're now outsourcing its creation!

If you're using tonic water or soda as a mixer, be sure to use a diet
version with 0g of carbs!

Cocktail Supplies

If you're mixing up drinks or creating fantastic cocktails, here are the carbohydrate counts for your non-alcoholic ingredients, such as olives, cherries, pineapple juice, and more.

These counts are all net carbs. The default unit of measure is an 8oz serving.

apple juice, unsweetened - 29g
Coca Cola - 30g
cranberry juice - 36g
cucumber slice - 0g
diet soda - 0g
grenadine syrup (1 Tbsp) - 13g
lemon juice (1oz) - 2.5g
lime juice (1oz) - 2.7g
maraschino cherry (1) - 2g
olive (1) - .5g
orange juice - 26g
pearl onion (1) - 0g
Pepsi Cola – 28g
pineapple juice - 34g

Tonic water comes in a number of carb levels - check your bottle to determine the carb count of the specific one you have chosen. Many people think because it says "water" that it has zero carbs - but that is usually not true.

Tips for Mixing Drinks

Many mixed drinks involve soda so probably the *most* important
thing you can do is get a bunch of Splenda-sweetened sodas in all
flavors for your house. Ginger Ale and Cola are two of the most
commonly used flavors. That way you can include those in your
cocktails without adding any sugar to the mix.

If you enjoy fruit juice cocktails, it might be time to train yourself
to enjoy other types. Fruit juices are incredibly high in sugar and
low in nutrients. Alternately, get the same flavors by using the
alcohol equivalent. If you like the flavor of orange, look for Grand
Marnier which is an orange flavored alcohol.

Flavored Vodkas

Sure, we know that straight vodka has 0g carbs and is great for mixed drinks. But how about all those flavored vodkas that are springing up?

Absolut
The Absolut website states, "Vodka contains 9.6 MJ (2300 kcal)/liter. ABSOLUT VODKA consists of almost exclusively alcohol and water and does not contain carbohydrates. This information is also valid for the flavored ABSOLUT vodkas."

It makes you wonder just what they are using as a flavoring, if it's not the natural fruit which would have sugars in it! When I wrote Absolut and asked them about this, here was their response:

"Our products contain no carbohydrates. Flavor suppliers produce aroma substances according to our recipe from natural ingredients. During this production process both sugar (carbohydrate) and colorings are extracted. The contents of sugar have been controlled several times and never has been detected."

Grey Goose
Grey Goose L'Orange - 0g carbs
Grey Goose La Poire - 0g carbs
Grey Goose Le Citron - 0g carbs
Grey Goose Vanilla - 0g carbs

If you have another style of flavored vodka that you enjoy, let me know and I'll research it to add it in. I think one could probably make the assumption that most flavored vodkas have zero carbs, though, based on the above information. Vodka makers seem to have figured out the technique for adding interesting flavors to their vodkas without causing any additional carbs. That's a good thing for us low carb dieters!

Smirnoff

Are you a fan of the Smirnoff drinks? Here is all of their nutritional information, including the carb counts!

Drink Name	calories	carbs	serving size
Smirnoff 80 proof	66	0	1 oz
Smirnoff 90.4 proof	74	0	1 oz
Smirnoff 100 proof	82	0	1 oz
Raspberry Twist	64	1.16	1 oz
Citrus Twist	60	0	1 oz
Green Apple Twist	66	1.56	1 oz
Cranberry Twist	66	1.56	1 oz
Orange Twist	65	0.64	1 oz
Vanilla Twist	63	0.96	1 oz
Orange Twisted	186	20.8	355 ml
Raspberry Twisted	182	20.2	355 ml
Green Apple Twisted	191	22.0	355 ml
Cranberry Twisted	184	20.4	355 ml
Sorbet Light	78	1.3	1.5 oz

Note the much larger serving size on the twisted offerings!

All Smirnoff drinks have zero protein and zero fat.

NOTE: Someone wrote me asking about the twisted drinks, if someone drinks 6 or more a day like soda, is this an issue. The answer is definitely *yes* not only in terms of the massive amounts of calories the person is taking in but also in terms of the alcohol content.

Doctors recommend the average woman drink a maximum of one alcoholic drink a day. Men can tolerate two. At higher levels, the person receives liver damage, brain damage, and other issues. It might not be readily apparent - but MRIs show the changes are happening.

Alcohol is a poison. Your body is not meant to ingest large amounts of it and work well.

Some people fall into the trap of thinking "oh it's sweet, therefore it's fun to drink." Sweet does not mean it's good for you. Quite the opposite. These drinks are 70 proof. That means they are 35% alcohol - or about *three times* the alcohol in a glass of wine. If someone drinks six "wine glasses" worth of Twisted a day, that's like drinking 18 glasses of wine in a day. I think we could all agree that would be extreme :).

Wine - Red

Red wine has been shown to prolong life, hold back cancer and heart disease as well as provide many other health benefits. Luckily, it's the perfect complement to the Atkins, South Beach, and other low carb diet plans!

You might think that grapes are full of sugar - but fermentation is when yeast eats sugar and turns it into carbon dioxide and alcohol. The reason the wine has alcohol is that sugar was destroyed. While there might be trace amounts of sugar left in the resulting wine, the primary reason for a calorie count in wine is the alcohol.

Wine, or any alcohol, is not appropriate for people in the first two weeks of a low carb diet. Part of the first two week process is evening out your blood sugar level, and alcohol lowers blood sugar levels. While this is good in general, you want to have *no* effects on your blood sugar levels during those first two weeks so that your body becomes stabilized.

Once those first two weeks are done, you should feel free to have a glass or two of wine as part of a healthy diet. A 5oz glass of red wine only has about 3.5g of carbs in it. Wine generally would not have sugar added to it, so you really don't have to worry about finding a "low sugar red".

The only wines to be cautious of are Late Harvest / Icewines - these are harvested late in the year and are not fully fermented, leaving sugar behind in the wine. These are normally white wines and are clearly labeled.

So enjoy red wine with your low carb lunch or dinner! The red wine will help enhance the flavor of your meal, it raises your good cholesterol levels to help offset any fat you're eating, it lowers chances of cancer, heart disease, strokes, ulcers, and more. Recent research shows that it helps prolong life in general.

In addition to my low carb website I also run a wine site, WineIntro. I've written content on wine for about fifteen years. If you have any questions about wine, health, and losing weight, let me know. I'm happy to help out!

This is a drink to toast to your health with!

Wine - White

White wine goes perfectly with many dishes - salads, chicken, fish. How well does white wine go with a low carb diet?

First, it's important to realize that ANY carb count you ever get is an approximation. If you say a tomato is 3.2g per half cup, that isn't true for EVERY tomato! Some tomatoes are sweet, some are less sweet. Some are dense, some are less dense. Eating healthy is about general guidelines, it is NOT about exact measurements. It is simply impossible.

So that being said, it is impossible to know how many carbs are in a Ridge Chardonnay vs a Tucker Pinot Grigio. Don't even bother trying. Plus, few people measure out their glass of wine with a measuring cup to get exactly the right volume into their wine glass. There are always going to be these issues in dieting. Your aim is to avoid the really bad things, aim for the really good things, and find a lifestyle you can maintain.

In general, white wine only has 3g of carbs per 5 oz serving. Compare that with red wine, which has about 3.5g of carbs per 5 oz serving. You can try to make guesstimates about a sweeter white wine having .5 more carbs than a less sweet white wine, but to be honest that's not worth worrying about. You should drink a wine you enjoy. You should never force yourself to drink a dryer wine to gain .5g of carb benefit. You probably burn that amount up using the corkscrew to open up the bottle.

Yes, you can say that "straight" alcohol like vodka or gin has 0g carbs. But on the other hand, wine has many health benefits and antioxidants that straight alcohol does not. So you gain more, in overall health, by going with wine.

Plus, wine really helps a meal taste better. It helps bring out the flavors in a meal. With so many low carb food items being white wine friendly - all of your fish, chicken, pork, vegetable recipes - this is a wonderful thing. You sit down at the table, pour a glass of wine, put on some soft music, and really savor your food. That helps you take longer to eat, appreciate your food more, and lose weight.

So I highly recommend having a glass of wine with each meal, unless of course your doctor has a reason to discourage this for your medical health. It is a great part of a low carb diet, and a great part of general healthy lifestyle.

Wine - Champagne and Sparkling

It's traditional to enjoy Champagne or sparkling wine at celebrations. Just how many carbs are in Champagne, to keep you on your low carb or Atkins diet?

You can't go by the calorie count. The calories in Champagne come from the alcohol, which is completely different than carbohydrates, proteins, or fats. Alcohol is the fourth type of substance your body is capable of metabolizing into energy. That's why many low carb diets warn you to avoid alcohol for the first two weeks - so that your body doesn't try to burn the alcohol instead of learning to burn primarily fats.

Since the process of fermentation is all about the yeast turning the sugars in grapes into alcohol, you don't have many natural sugars in the wine, either. However, Champagne is special because it goes through a secondary fermentation - the one that gives it its signature bubbles. Wineries also add a "dosage" to the Champagne at the end, to add flavor to it. This means that there is actually sugar in a finished bottle of Champagne, where a normal wine has little to none.

The actual carb amount varies wildly from maker to maker, and from year to year, depending on the grapes used, the yeast used, the dosage used, and more. Wineries don't check for carb counts so really it's best just to go with a basic idea that a non-sweet Champagne has around 5g per glass and a very sweet sparkling wine has around 10g per glass. To try to narrow it down more than that is pretty impossible.

Here is a list of common types of Champagne and sparkling wines you will find, ordered from very dry (non-sweet) to very sweet:

Extra Brut
Brut
Extra Dry
Sec
Demi-Sec
Sec
Sekt (German)
Asti Spumanti (Italian)
Prosecco (Italian)

So if you are aiming for the lowest amount of carbs in your sparkling wine, you want to look for the extra brut styles. You would want to avoid Prosecco and Asti Spumanti, both which are very sweet.

Whisky / Whiskey / Bourbon

Whiskey and Whisky are both very similar drinks, made in different locations. Pretty much every whiskey on the market - from Crown Royal to Glenfiddich Scotch - is zero carbs. Scotch is a specific type of whiskey - i.e. whiskey that comes from Scotland. Bourbon is another kind of whisky - i.e. whisky that comes from Kentucky.

In general, whiskies from Scotland and Canada are spelled "whisky" while others are spelled "whiskey". Whiskies from Scotland are called "Scotch".

Bourbon is a little trickier. There is a Bourbon country in Kentucky and most whiskeys from Kentucky are called "bourbon" after this region. However, a tiny amount of whiskeys made elsewhere in the US call themselves bourbon because they feel they offer the same style.

Whether the drinks are called Scotch, Bourbon, Whisky, or Whiskey, they are all the same basic thing - fermented grain alcoholic beverages.

While I can say with great certainty that every whiskey *should* be 0g of carbs per serving, here are the ones I have specifically verified for people:

Bushmills Irish Whiskey – 0g
- a traditional Irish whiskey

Canadian Mist - 0g
- a Canadian whisky made from corn and barley. Made in Ontario.

Canadian R&R Whisky - 0g
- a cheap one from Canada, it is just alcohol. I can't even find a
website for this one though.

Chivas Regal Scotch Whisky - 0g carbs
- from Scotland, a blended whisky

Cougar Bourbon - reported direct from Foster's PR people for
100ml:
- Cougar Bourbon 0.0g
- Cougar Bourbon and Cola 8.7g
- Cougar XS 0.0g
- Cougar Zero (pre mix) 0.05g

Crown Royal Whisky - 0g carbs, 0g fat, 97 calories per 1.5oz
- from Canada, a blend of corn, barley and rye

Canadian Club Whisky - 0g carbs, 0g fat, 96 calories per 1.5oz
- from Canada, uses corn, barley, rye and rye malt

Early Times - 65 calories, zero carbohydrates, and is gluten-free
- reported by the EarlyTimes crew. Per ounce.

Fireball Whisky -
- There are 11 carbs and 108 calories in 1.5 fluid ounce of Fireball
Whiskey. Straight from their PR people.

Glenfiddich Scotch Whisky - 0g carbs
- from Scotland, best-selling single malt Scotch. Made solely from
malted barley

Glenmorangie Scotch Whisky - 0g carbs
- from Scotland, mentioned in "The Highlander". Made solely from malted barley
from their staff: "The calorific value of whisky at 40% abv [alcohol by volume] is 220 cals/100ml, so I'm afraid it doesn't come under the heading of a diet drink, however there are no carbohydrates in whisky so you'll be OK if you are following the Atkins diet."

Grant's Scotch Whisky - verifying but they should be 0g

Jack Daniels Tennessee Whiskey - 0g carbs, 0g fat, 72 calories per 1oz
- from Tennessee of course. It's not Bourbon because it's not from Kentucky!

Jameson Irish whiskey - 0g carbs
- established in Dublin Ireland

Jim Beam Bourbon - 0g carbs
- Bourbon, from Clemont, Kentucky :) 100 calories per shot, 80 proof

Johnnie Walker Scotch Whisky - 0g carbs
- from Scotland, a blended variety. They use 27 different distilleries.

Kentucky Deluxe Blended Whiskey - 0g carbs
- From Heaven Hill Distillers: "Thank you for your inquiry regarding Kentucky Deluxe whiskey. Kentucky Deluxe 80-proof whiskey has 98 Calories per Standard Serving Size of 1.5 fluid ounce. It contains no carbohydrates."

Dr. McGillicuddy's® Fireball Canadian whisky - 0g carbs
- also 69 calories, 0g fat. 100% Canadian whisky, 66 proof, cinnamon flavors

Maker's Mark - 0g carbs
- "There are no carbs and appx 70 calories per one ounce of
Maker's Mark."

Seagram's 7 Crown Whiskey - 0g carbs
- This has 40% alcohol, 97 calories per shot.

Southern Comfort - 3g carbs
- history is it was first created in Louisiana. Technically a peach
flavored liqueur

If you have another type of whiskey or whisky that you love,
please let me know, and I will research it to add in to this list!

There are many fun recipes that involve whiskey (and its relatives)
which are rather low carb.

Remember that your body processes alcohol before it moves on to
carbs. If you drink too much alcohol, then your body will turn all
carbs you ingest into fat. Read the articles linked to below for more
information!

NOTE: There are factions who get riled up over Bourbon
definitions. They feel anything can be a Bourbon as long as it
follows a Kentucky recipe. This is sort of like the Champagne
argument, that Champagne can be made outside of France as long
as it uses the Champagne method. However, I happen to side with
the people who say that certain names are associated with certain
locations. I do not think a Thailand whiskey should be called a
Bourbon.

Summary

Knowing what you are eating is the first step towards making healthier choices. Once you realize which foods are full of sugar and which are not, you can start sorting out your meals and deciding to eat items which will benefit your health.

This process is not about memorizing exact numbers. Rather, it is about getting a sense of which foods are better than others and making your choices accordingly.

For thousands of recipes and tips on eating healthy foods, be sure to visit LowCarb.BellaOnline.com

Enjoy a healthier you!

If you enjoyed this book, please leave a review on Amazon, GoodReads, and whatever other sites you participate in. Together we can bring low carb goodness to those who treasure good health and delicious food!

Appendices

It's good to read these appendices when you first get the book, so you get a grounding in how to eat and cook in a healthy manner. After that, refer to these sections whenever you need a refresher on how these systems work!

About Carbohydrates

No matter what sort of healthy eating system you are on, it is important to understand what you are eating. Just what are carbohydrates, and how do they affect your body?

Carbohydrates are one of the four main types of energy that your body is physically able to burn for fuel. The other three energy types are fats, proteins, and alcohols. This is basic human construction and biology.

The Carbohydrate is the easiest thing for your body to burn, so if your body has the choice of burning through that Ring Ding you ate or the fat on your thighs it'll burn the Ring Ding - and probably add more extra fat to your thighs afterwards, too. On the other hand, if you eat fats or proteins, your body has to first convert those things into carbohydrates, and then use the carbohydrates for energy. So even if you eat more *calories* on a fat-rich diet, you still lose more weight, because your body is doing extra work to use those fats.

Living on an alcohol diet is not recommended for many reasons :)

There are three types of carbohydrates:

Simple Carbohydrates - Sugars

Sugars include the white table sugar stuff (sucrose) as well as fruit sugars (fructose), milk sugars (lactose) and so on. Sugar is *very* easy for your body to use, so your body doesn't have to do much work in order to take in sugar and turn it into fat.

Sugar spikes your body's blood sugar levels, causing large mood swings. When the sugar rush is gone (and all the excess sugar is packed into your tummy for storage as fat) then your body gets hungry immediately and craves more food. It is these swings and the easy-to-fat cycle that low carb diets are trying to break.

When Man was evolving, he did not have Yodels and chocolate-covered donuts hanging on his trees. The amount of sugar modern man eats - in everything from breakfast cereals to breads and TV dinners - is staggering. No matter what style of healthy eating you choose to follow, it undoubtedly recommends cutting out soda, junk food, and excess sugar.

Complex Carbohydrates - Starches

Starches are those rich carbohydrates found in bread, potatoes, pasta, and French fries. Starches cause the exact same problems that sugars do. They spike your blood sugar levels, giving you a quick boost of energy, but setting you up for a big *loss* of energy once the spike is gone. You also feel hungry again after the spike because the blood sugar levels drop so drastically.

Many foods such as Chinese food are cooked in very starch-rich sauces, which cause the hungry-shortly-afterwards issues.

Dietary Fiber

If you look at a nutrition panel on processed food, you'll see that Dietary Fiber is listed under the total carbohydrate listing. Fiber is a *very* healthy thing to eat and helps keep your digestion system regular. Eating fiber daily is very important to your health. Better yet - fiber does *not* impact your weight situation at all.

Fiber doesn't turn into fat or energy - it just goes through your stomach and intestines, helping to keep it clean. So in short, fiber does *not* count as a carb. Technically it is part of the carbohydrate family, but in terms of impact on your body, fiber is not processed at all.

It's important to be clear about a key issue involving carbohydrates. Participating in a low carb lifestyle is **not** about avoiding vegetables. It is about avoiding *foods that are high in junk carbohydrates*. So that means staying away from things like white bread, potatoes, pasta, candied yams, and the like. I'm not sure there is any dietician that would tell you that eating white bread *is* healthy for you.

It might be true that high-energy foods like potatoes were necessary for farmers in the 1700s who were out in the field working hard. These intrepid souls needed a supply of high-powered energy to get through the day. But for the typical person in the modern developed world, that high powered energy simply equates to thick thighs and a round stomach.

Effective Carbs vs Total Carbs

When you look at the back nutrition panel of a processed food, it lists Total Carbohydrates. But then it lists dietary fiber and sugars. What is the final, effective carb count?

First, carbs are the white sugars, the starchy pastas and potatoes in life. To reiterate an important point, avoiding carbs is **not** about avoid avoiding vegetables. You should eat large amounts of healthy vegetables on a low carb diet. Avoiding carbs is really about avoiding unhealthy sugars and starches.

The point of counting carbs is to figure out how many carbs in a given dish will have an impact on your blood sugar levels and your potential fat gain or loss. You want to keep your blood sugar levels even, so you do not have hunger cravings or interrupt your fat loss. You normally want to keep your carb intake below a certain number that for you represents the amount of carbs your body needs to get energy for the day. That way the remaining energy will come from your fat cells that you are trying to get rid of.

Because of that aim, the only carbs you count are the ones that can **turn into fat**. Any carb that just goes in one end and out the other end doesn't count towards your Effective Carbs, because those carbs will not effect at all how your body gets energy or burns fat.

Dietary Fiber

One of the values listed on a nutrition panel is dietary fiber. While fiber is a carb, it is **not** used by the body for energy and is not processed. Fiber is *critical* to keeping your digestive system clean and working smoothly. Luckily for us, it doesn't get turned into energy or fat, so it is non-impactful as far as your weight loss goes.

So if for example the zucchini chips bag has 8g of carbohydrates - but 4g of those are dietary fiber - it actually only has 4g (8-4) of *meaningful* or effective carbs. If you ate a serving of chips, you would only count that you had ingested 4g of carbs.

Sugar Alcohols

Sugar Alcohols are often not counted by low carb dieters. This is because sugar alcohols flow through your system without being processed. Your body doesn't recognize them as sugar. It should be noted that some people are sensitive to sugar alcohols, and have 'gastric distress' when eating them. It's always wise to start with a very small portion of a food containing sugar alcohols, to see how your body reacts to them.

Glycemic Index

The glycemic index of a food is in essence how quickly the body absorbs the sugars found in food. Examples of foods with high glycemic indexes are white potatoes and white bread.

While many different types of foods contain sugars in them, in some cases the sugars are very slow to be absorbed. Your body might not even absorb those sugars before they pass through your system. In other cases, however, the sugars get into your body with amazing speed and get stored away in the fat cells for later use.

If you eat foods with high glycemic indexes, the "easily available" sugar in them triggers your body to release insulin. Insulin tells your fat cells to start absorbing all the sugar to get it out of your blood system. Once the wave of sugar is gone, your body goes down into a 'trough', with low insulin and blood sugar levels - and you get hungry again. The binge-eating then continues.

A good example of high glycemic index food is Chinese Food, in the traditional US take-out way. I have to note here that *authentic* traditional Chinese food is quite healthy, with fresh fish stock and vegetables. However, the way US people tend to eat Chinese food, they eat piles of white rice, chicken soaked in a sugar-sauce and breaded dumplings filled with sugar-mix. All of that food has an incredibly high glycemic index. The body is overwhelmed with sugar. It releases massive amounts of insulin and all of that sugar goes straight into fat cells. And then the body reacts to the subsequent "sharp lowering" of blood sugar levels as a danger sign and becomes hungry again.

While low carb diets were among the first to point out the hazards of high glycemic foods, most other diet systems have now followed suit and recognize that foods such as white bread and white rice have lots of sugar and very few nutrients. Every diet plan I've studied is now recommending that people switch to the healthier varieties of whole wheat bread and brown rice.

In a "shorthand" way, foods with high carb counts usually have high glycemic index counts as well. But to understand more *why* you are avoiding high carb counts, it's important to learn about the glycemic index, and to begin to look for that information on the foods you eat. Hopefully soon this information will be printed on every label you pick up and read!

Low Carb Food List

Here is an overview of the types of foods you can expect to be eating on a low carb diet. It will give you a general idea of the lifestyle that many of us enjoy, day in and day out, as our healthy way of eating.

Meats/Fish
Just about every meat and fish has 0g of carbs. The exception is processed deli meats which often have not only carbs but nitrates. Liver is also carb-rich. In general, though, every meal should have a serving of meat, fish, or some other form of protein in it. Protein is critical for healthy body functioning.

Vegetables
It is extremely important to eat your vegetables! They are chock-full of nutrients. Some of the lowest carb veggies are broccoli, cauliflower, cabbage, asparagus, celery, cucumber, lettuce, radishes, and spinach. You can eat all vegetables in moderation, but stay away from corn, peas, and potatoes! All are full of carbs. Save those for treats later on.

Fruits
While an Apple a Day might keep the doctor away, it's also very sugary. That is true for many fruits. Yes, enjoy those berries that are full of antioxidants, but don't build your menus around fruits. There are far better ways to get most of your nutrients. Fruits are best as an occasional dessert.

Milk, Dairy, and Eggs
Many people become lactose-intolerant as they age. The enzymes that babies possess to digest milk often fades away in adults. It's good to cut down your milk consumption for the first two weeks, and see how your body likes it. You might very well feel far better

without it! An egg or two a day is a great way to get protein into you.

Nuts and Seeds
What tasty treats! Instead of pretzels and chips, pour out a handful of nuts and enjoy. They are healthy for you.

Healthy humans should drink a *lot* of water - at least 8 glasses a day. Many times when you think you are hungry you may actually be thirsty. Keep a glass of water by your side, and you'll find that you reach for it often ... far more often than you might have guessed!

Preparing to Start

Any lifestyle change requires some preparation. If your home is full of sugary soda and chocolate, and you work in a donut bakery, you could find it exceedingly difficult to work on a low carb diet. The environment you're in will not support you in your goal.

So take a week before you begin your diet to prepare your house, your pantry, your fridge. These tips will help you build a world around you that supports healthy eating. Tell your family and friends that you are planning on eating more healthy foods, and ask for their support.

If your kids only drink sugary soda, it might be time to get them out of that habit while you're changing your own lifestyle! The incidence of childhood obesity is at an all time high. With the plethora of sugar-free products on the market nowadays, there is little excuse to be ruining your teeth and health with the sugar-filled ones.

Stocking a Low Carb Pantry

You're getting ready to go with a low carb diet. Here's how to stock your pantry and your fridge to give your diet the best possible chance of success.

First, *clear out the junk food!!* Get rid of the candy, chocolate, ice cream, and other unhealthy food items. No matter *what* method you want to use to lose some weight, that junk food has to go.

Now, to get some better options in the house.

Water
Water is the most important thing on *any* diet, a low carb diet included. You should drink at least eight glasses of water a day. This may seem like a lot, but if you keep a glass of water by you, you'd be surprised just how much you drink as a matter of course!

Whether it's a fridge that gives fresh water, a pitcher on your desk, a Brita water filter in the fridge, or bottled water, get that water into you.

Lots of Cheese
Whatever types of cheese you enjoy, get a variety of blocks of cheese into the house. Cheese is a great, tasty treat. It provides calcium which is important for strong bones and teeth.

Greens and Broccoli
We have found bag-o-broccoli and bag-o-baby-spinach to be greatly useful. The more quick-and-easy veggies you have around, the more likely you are to eat some.

Snacking Veggies
Whether it's carrot sticks, celery sticks, cucumber slices, zucchini slices, cauliflower in dip, get a variety of veggie snacks in the

house. You don't have to eat these things plain - there are a wide
variety of cheeses, sauces, and combos that will make these items
taste delicious.

Fresh Meats

Avoid processed sandwich meats - they're full of nitrates. Think
like a European, and swing by the market on the way home. Is the
fresh, preservative-free roast beef on sale? How about some
preservative-free turkey breast? Grab some shrimp for a cocktail
and get smoked salmon for breakfast.

Tuna Fish

Tuna fish is very good for you, to help you stock up on the
important omega-3 oils. Just make sure not to eat it daily – you
have to balance the good of the tuna with the variety offered by
other food items.

Eat those Vitamins

No matter how you eat nowadays, you need your vitamins. Very
few human beings in this life get all the nutrients they need from
what they eat. There was a report of a college student in California
getting scurvy because all he ate was a 'normal American diet'!
Get those vitamins into you.

You'll find very quickly on a low carb diet that you will rarely be
hungry - your body will find enough 'fuel' within its own fat cells.
However, when you begin any change of lifestyle, much of the
challenge is in your mind. This is definitely true with an eating
change. You don't want to *feel* like you have little to eat. So the
more healthy, yummy food you have around you, the "safer" you
will feel.

Quick Cooking Low Carb Food List

It's time to get shopping. Print this out and bring it with you to the grocery store! Choose your favorites, plus add one or two "new things" each time you shop too, to explore new foods. You might be surprised how tasty it can be to eat fresh food!

Meats/Fish

Just about every meat and fish has 0g of carbs. Do not eat processed meats, hot dogs, or liver. Get protein into each meal. It is necessary for your body to thrive.

__ Hard boiled eggs
__ Pre-cooked Chicken Wings (deserves special mention, these are *perfect* snacks)
__ Nitrate-free luncheon meats (turkey, roast beef, etc.)
__ Cans of tunafish (get the chunk lite, not the white/albacore)
__ Smoked Salmon

Cheese

Cheese is full of calcium and other good nutrients.

__ Cheddar Cheese (great for sprinkling over salads)
__ Swiss
__ Mozzarella (make an eggplant pizza)
__ Gouda

Vegetables

It is extremely important to eat your vegetables! They are chock-full of important nutrients. Try to have a veggie or two at each meal, and extra veggies for snacks. Learn new, fun veggies recipes!

__ Alfalfa Sprouts
__ Bamboo Shoots
__ Bean Sprouts
__ Broccoli
__ Cabbage
__ Cauliflower
__ Celery
__ Collard Greens
__ Cucumber
__ Lettuce
__ Mushrooms (try all sorts of varieties!)
__ Radishes
__ Sauerkraut
__ Spinach
__ Tomato
__ Water Chestnuts
__ Zucchini

Other Food Items

These items will help ensure you can make a variety of recipes, to keep your menu interesting and tasty.

__ Olive Oil
__ Vinegar
__ Butter
__ Splenda sweetener
__ Sour Cream
__ Diet soda (with Splenda), bottled water, low carb iced teas
__ Olives
__ Nuts
__ Berries

I'll note here that ideally you will want to ease soda out of your life – but as you get started it's OK to take that process gradually.

Herbs

Make sure your spice cabinet is up to date! You will find it amazing how flavorful your food can be when it's made fresh and flavored with delicious spices.

Must Have Low Carb Basic Ingredients

If you're on a low carb diet, there are certain items that you simply MUST have in your kitchen to be able to whip up quick and easy recipes. Here's the list.

Oils
Butter
Mayonnaise
Olive Oil

Spices
Garlic Powder
Minced Garlic
Mustard
Onion Powder
Pepper
Salt

Canned Things
Mushrooms
Water Chestnuts

In addition, I recommend keeping a pack or two of low carb tortillas around. They are perfect for making wraps for lunch, breakfast rolls in the morning, and all sorts of other recipes. They're the one "prepared" low carb item that I use almost daily!

Must Have Low Carb Spice List

Spices can turn a bland dish into a delicious favorite. Be sure to keep these herbs and spices in the fridge - you'll be using them quite a bit!

Note that herbs and spices have an effective life of six months but are only harvested yearly. So keep them in the door of your fridge and date them, but don't bother buying them until a year later even though they'll be past their prime by then. Chances are that the stuff you see in the supermarket is from the same year as yours is!

Basil
Known to the Greeks, Basil came to Europe by way of India. It has a rich aroma and is used in vegetable, fish, and salad dishes.

Dill
Dill is an ancient herb used in preserving many types of foods. It's perfect for fish, egg, and cheese dishes.

Garlic Powder
Garlic is incredibly healthy for you and is used in just about every cuisine on the planet. Some people would say that you can use garlic in just about any dish you make :).

Ginger
Ginger has been used in Asia for thousands of years. It has been proven to help with upset stomachs. It goes wonderfully with vegetable and meat dishes.

Oregano
The classic Italian herb adds an aromatic flavor to any dish. Oregano is great with veggies, cheese, and salads.

Go light on the salt and pepper - and invest in a pepper mill that grinds the peppercorns up when you need them. Fill it with one of those four-color or five-color peppercorn blends, and see just how much more flavor is added to your recipes!

Tips and Tricks

Our entire modern day culture is geared around stuffing as much food into your face as possible, supersizing your meals, and eating foods that are high in sugar and low in nutrients. This, as you can imagine, is not a healthy way to live.

Part of what you're doing on a low carb diet is eating more healthy foods. The other thing you're doing is learning to eat in a more healthy manner. You get the best results when combining both of these concepts together.

Here are tips and tricks to help you eat more healthily, and lose weight more easily.

Clearing your Plate Leads to Obesity

In an amazing study done by the American Institute for Cancer Research, people would mindlessly clear their entire plate of food - even if it held far more than they actually wanted to eat. Studies show that people eat up to 56% more calories than they normally would, just because it's sitting on the plate before them.

In the study, the researchers fed their patients varying plate sizes of macaroni and cheese. The patients would tend to eat the entire plate worth - no matter how much was on it. While they would report feeling "full" from the small plate, when given the large plate on another day they would eat it all up as well - and over half of them didn't even realize they had eaten almost 50% additional food. They had simply been trained by our culture to eat "whatever was on the plate" and not think about whether they were full or hungry.

This "eat everything regardless of how full I am" mindset has become a huge health problem at restaurants, especially fast food restaurants. With large portions and "biggy sized" meals, consumers go right past being "full" and fill themselves with hundreds, if not thousands, of extra calories and carbs.

It can be equally bad at home. Many families are brought up with the "more food is good" mentality, especially those who remember back to days when food was scarce. So they pile up the plates with food, actively push family members to eat more and then insist people not leave any food behind on the plate. All of these activities drive people not only to overeat on that one occasion - but actively alter their bodies to cause them to overeat in the future.

The stomach is an amazingly adaptable organ and stretches to accommodate the extra food. This means that the stomach now needs more food to feel "full" the next time the person eats, and the problem gets worse and worse.

As consumers get more overweight, they demand larger portions from restaurants, which respond in order to please their customers. A 2002 study in the Journal of the American Dietetic Association found that the average order of fries weighs 7.1oz today. In 1955, a person ordering fries would receive 2.4oz. It's not that restaurants were *stingy* before. It's that we as consumers expect "lots of food" - and then gobble it down whether we feel that hungry or not.

Many studies show that it is this trend of constant overeating that has contributed to current weight problems. Research shows that in countries where people eat slowly and stop when they are full, the population maintains a healthy weight even when eating "unhealthy" and fattening items. They might eat that chocolate cake, but they just have a little of it and stop when they are full.

So in short, use small plates, take small portions, and eat slowly. You can *always go back for more*. Low carb dieting insists you eat until you are full. You should never be hungry. But do not *stuff* yourself. Give yourself time to notice you are full, and when you are, stop. The remains on the plate can go in the fridge for later.

Slow Music Reduces your Appetite

It is amazing how our body is tied into the signals it hears. Try playing slow music while you eat - it can reduce your intake by up to 40%!

Many people tend to eat quickly in our fast-paced society. It can take a while for the stomach's "I'm Full" message to reach the brain. If you are eating too quickly, you may eat another half a meal before you realize that you were actually full a while ago. The extra calories you packed in go right to your hips as fat.

Be sure to keep a full glass of water by your plate, even if you're drinking something else with your meal. Reach for a drink often. Taking the drink will add breaks into your eating and help slow the pace of the meal.

By listening to gentle music while you eat, you lower your stress levels and eat more slowly. You actually hear your body's message of "I'm full now" instead of continuing to push more food into your mouth. The result? Less calories in, the same amount of fullness, and your weight becomes more healthy!

Slow Music Suggestions:

CLASSICAL

* Sleeper's Wake - Bach

* Pachelbel's Canon - Pachelbel

* Fall 2 / Adagio molto - Vivaldi

OLDIES

* Surfer Girl - Beach Boys

* Summertime - Billie Holiday

* Something so Right - Paul Simon

MODERN

* More than Words - Extreme

* One Man's Dream - Yanni

* May it Be - Enya

* You Belong to Me - Jason Wade

Of course, go with whatever style of music you enjoy the most! Create a dinnertime play list, and cut your calorie intake by 40% without even trying.

Reduce Stress to Reduce Carb Cravings

Often your body craves sugar and carbs when it's feeling stressed out or worn down. Your body does this even though it knows the post-carb crash will be worse than what you began with!

Studies have shown that just about any person who takes time to unwind after a long day, or even takes a nap, will eat fewer carbs when they sit down to dinner. Their body does not crave that sugar-rush to pick them up - they have already unwound naturally. The fewer carbs and sugar equate to less pounds packed on the hips and stomach as a result!

Our bodies are genetically trained to hold onto weight when under stress. In order to lose weight, you also have to remove that stress, so your body releases the fat.

The main culprit is a substance known as *cortisol*. When you are feeling stressed your body releases cortisol into your system. The cortisol gives you a boost of energy to deal with that stress. However, since our bodies were developed to think stress = running top speed from an attacking wolf, the cortisol also boosts your hunger levels, assuming that you'll need to replenish your energy stores before the next attack.

Of course, in modern times most of our stress comes when we are sitting at our desk. So we get the stress induced hormones, but then also the stress induced hunger cravings. So we eat - and get heavy.

Note that lack of sleep also causes an increase in levels of cortisol - so if you skimp on sleep, you make this problem worse.

If you are looking to change your weight situation, a *key* ingredient could be to lower your stress levels. You can't control the outside world, but you *can* control your reactions to it. Set aside time for ample sleep. Set aside time for relaxation, whether it's fifteen minute meditations before breakfast or a half hour fun TV show in the evening. Make this a critical part of every day. You and your health are worth it.

Be sure to pay attention to your body's energy levels during the day. Drink eight glasses of water, take your vitamins, and be sure to snack on healthy foods so that you never go more than 3-4 hours between meals. That should keep your energy levels up so that when you approach the main meals you eat what is healthy for you - and not to satisfy short term cravings!

About the Author

Thank you so much for sharing a part of your life's journey with me! Bob and I have followed a low carb lifestyle since June 2003. We have enjoyed every day of it. Bob does the cooking, and I do the writing.

Low carb is a way of life which tantalizes the taste buds and provides an infinite supply of options. You can feast on filet mignon with asparagus. You can delight your exotic side with sashimi and a fresh seaweed salad. Delve into comfort food with a rich ratatouille. Take a virtual vacation to Alaska with smoked salmon for breakfast.

I am online daily to answer questions and provide support. Join whichever community best complements your lifestyle!

Facebook:
https://www.facebook.com/BellaOnlineLowCarb

Forum:
https://forums.bellaonline.com/ubbthreads.php/forums/221/1/Low_Carb

I look forward to talking with you!

Low Carb Reference Books

Here's my library of low carb reference books to help you on your low carb lifestyle. Let me know if you'd like to see any other topics covered!

Free Books

All of these books should be available for free from all platforms.

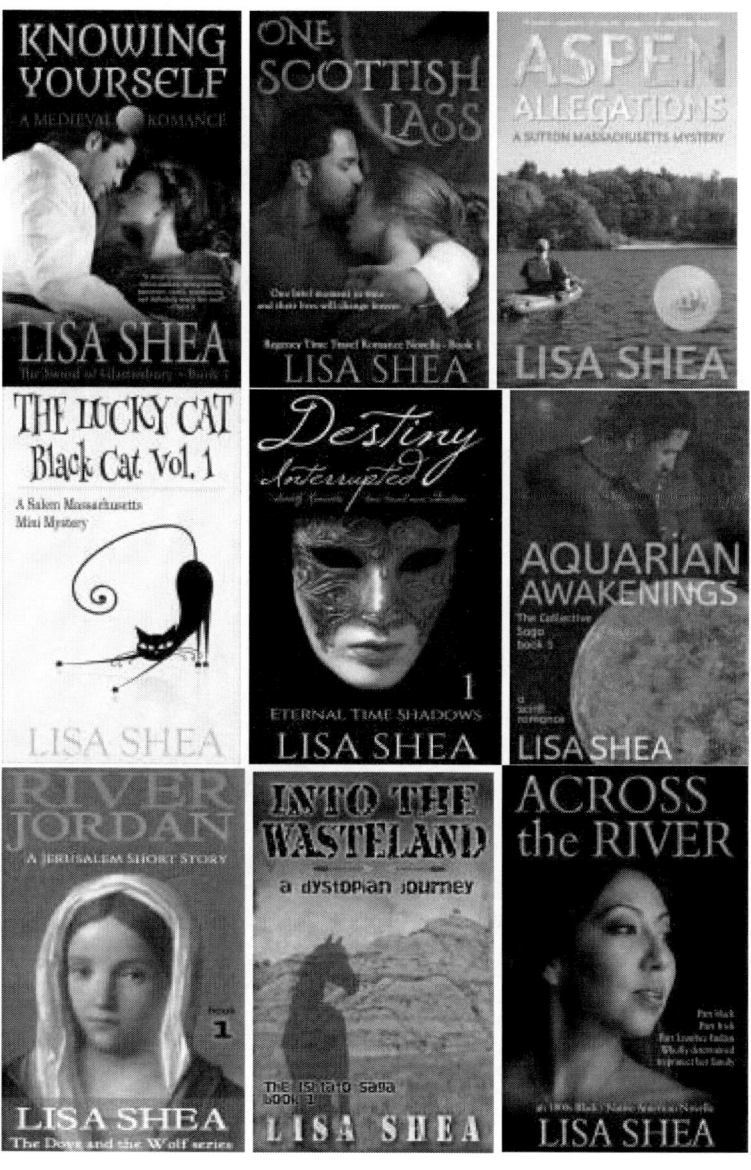

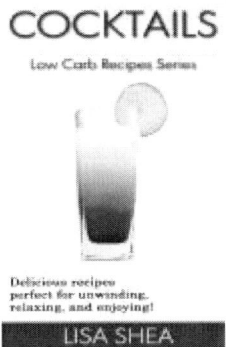

I may have added more free books since releasing this list here. For the most up to date version, be sure to visit:

http://www.lisashea.com/freebooks/

Thank you for supporting the cause!
Be the change you wish to see in the world.

Manufactured by Amazon.ca
Acheson, AB

33848861R00063